Mr. Hermit Miser

and the Neighborly Pumpkin

Christine Noble Govan
Illustrated by Anne Merriman Peck

Smidgen Press

Mr. Hermit Miser and the Neighborly Pumpkin

Christine Noble Govan | illustrations by Anne Merriman Peck
Edition copyright © 2022 by Smidgen Press | SmidgenPress.com

Contains unabridged public domain text by Christine N. Govan originally published in 1949. The body of this work is unedited, unrevised material and, as such, may contain outdated ideas and terminology. Smidgen Press and its employees and contractors are not responsible for any views expressed in this book.

Cover & recipe designs by Terri Shown
Contributions by JacQueline V. Roe
Book typeset by Skinner Book Services

Library of Congress Control Number: 2022920353

ISBNs | the parchment edition
     978-1-950536-37-5 (paperback)
     978-1-950536-38-2 (hardback)
the green edition
     978-1-950536-39-9 (paperback)
     978-1-950536-40-5 (hardback)

ALL THE HOUSES in Gillygreen Lane were painted green and white. All except Mr. Hermit Miser's. It wasn't painted at all.

All the windows in the green and white houses on Gillygreen Lane had flower boxes in them except the windows in the last house — which was Mr. Hermit Miser's. It had rags stuffed in the windows to keep the wind out.

All the cats in Gillygreen Lane were plump and clean. They slept on the doorsteps in the summer and by the warm fire in the winter. All but Mr. Hermit Miser's cat. It was thin and its fur was in patches. It slept on the roof and spat at people.

All the yards in Gillygreen Lane were trim and neat, with beds of bright flowers. All except the yard at the end of the street. This one was Mr. Hermit Miser's. It had only weeds. And the weeds were never cut unless the policeman, Mr. Snoopstagel, came by on his bicycle and said, "Cut those weeds at once or we will fine you!" (Because of the mosquitoes and things, you see.)

Then Mr. Hermit Miser would cut his weeds. He always cut them himself, for he would never pay a small boy to do it. He would cut them with awful thwacks and swacks, as if he were fighting Mr. Snoopstagel. Then he would go into his tumble-down house and let the weeds grow some more. He hoped that winter would cut them down before *he* had to do it again.

One spring day Mr. Hermit Miser came out into his yard. Right in the very middle of his lawn he saw two sturdy green leaves. He walked over and stared at the green leaves a long time. Then he went back into the house.

The next day Mr. Hermit Miser came out and looked at his lawn. *Four* green leaves and a little curly tail were growing there. He meant to cut them down, but the sickle was in the cellar. Anyway, it was rusty, so he put off doing it.

The next day Mr. Hermit Miser went out and looked at his lawn. There were *eight* leaves and four tiny tails. And the stem on which the leaves were growing had grown to at least a foot long. It lay along the ground like a vine.

This pleased Mr. Hermit Miser very much because he liked most of all to get something for nothing. He decided not to cut down the leaves.

Every morning when he got up he went out to look at his vine. Every morning there were eight or ten more leaves, and a lot more of the stem, and dozens of little new curly tails. Best of all, Mr. Miser saw that if the vine kept on growing at this rate he could just forget all about Mr. Snoopstagel. There wouldn't be any weeds to cut this year. The vine would cover them all up and keep them smothered out.

Mr. Hermit Miser looked almost pleasant nowadays when he sat on his porch and watched his quick-growing vine.

One day when Mr. Hermit Miser came out to look at the vine he found three beautiful golden blossoms on it. Then Mr. Hermit Miser actually smiled, for he knew that not only would the vine keep the weeds down but that someday he would have pumpkins, maybe two or three, on the vine. If there was one thing in the world that Mr. Hermit Miser liked, it was rich, spicy, luscious, crisp pumpkin pie.

Now one day Mr. Hermit Miser went out into his yard to look at his fine pumpkin vine. The stem and the bright leaves and the curly tails of the vine had grown in every direction. They had gone through the rickety fence on Mr. Miser's place where some of the slats were out. They had even come out in Mrs. Burman's yard next door.

Mrs. Burman always said that she just couldn't stand Mr. Miser because he wouldn't paint his house. He wouldn't cut his weeds, and he wouldn't patch his fence or mend his windows. Worst of all, he was mean to his cat, and that made Mrs. Burman very, very angry.

Mr. Miser didn't like Mrs. Burman, either.

When he saw that his beautiful pumpkin vine had gone through his fence and was growing in Mrs. Burman's yard, he made up his mind that he would go right over to get it. So he went around to Mrs. Burman's front gate. He walked down the neat brick walk to her trim little back yard. He bent over to pick up his naughty pumpkin vine and put it back into his own yard.

BUT just as he leaned over, he heard Mrs. Burman's screen door slam and Mrs. Burman cry, "Hermit Miser! What are you doing in my back yard? Get out of here! Scat!" And she came towards him, shaking her broom at him.

Mr. Miser was furious! He jumped up and down and shook his fist at Mrs. Burman.

"Mrs. Burman!" he said, and his voice was rusty because he hardly ever spoke to anybody. "Mrs. Burman. I've come for my own property — and I mean to take it back with me!"

"Wait a bit," she said, and she, too, stooped over and looked at the vine.

"It has put down roots," she said. "What grows in my own yard is mine. I just dare you to touch it!"

So Mr. Hermit Miser had to go home and leave his pumpkin vine growing in Mrs. Burman's yard. And Mrs. Burman watered it until it grew and grew and put out almost as many leaves and curly tails and yellow blossoms as Mr. Miser's part of the vine.

Mr. Hermit Miser was so busy watching the part of the vine that grew in Mrs. Burman's yard that he forgot his own vine.

One day, after the rain, Mr. Hermit Miser walked across the part of his yard that was left showing, and he saw that the pumpkin vine had burst through the fence on three other sides. It was now growing in Mrs. Burman's yard to the south. It was growing in Mrs. Brown's yard to the east and in Miss Pitcher's yard to the north. *And* — this made Mr. Miser hopping mad — the vine had walked out of the rusty front gate, which wouldn't shut because it needed mending. It was crawling right across the road. Anybody who came along could pick the pumpkins from it — if it ever had any pumpkins.

Mr. Miser saw his pumpkin vine running away down the street. He saw that it would soon be just anybody's pumpkin vine. This made him *so* mad that he could hardly *see*! Mr. Miser dashed out of the gate to pull up his vine and bring it back into the yard again.

Now just about this time Mr. Snoopstagel came by on his bicycle to see if Mr. Miser had cut his weeds. Mr. Snoopstagel rode along thinking how he would speak rather sharply to Mr. Miser. Just then he caught sight of Mr. Miser's yard and the great upright green leaves with the beautiful golden blossoms showing through.

Mr. Snoopstagel was so surprised that he forgot what he was doing. He pushed down on the pedals of the bicycle as hard as he could. At that moment Mr. Miser rushed out of the front gate, right into Mr. Snoopstagel's path.

There was a terrible THUMP and a squeaking of bicycle tires. For a minute there was a sort of pin wheel of bicycle, Snoopstagel, Miser, and dust, all wound around with green vine.

When the dust settled, the bicycle lay in one place. Mr. Snoopstagel lay in another. The vine looked as if it had been chewed by a cow. And Mr. Miser was crumpled up against Miss Pitcher's fence, groaning and holding his foot in his hand.

Miss Pitcher came screaming. Mrs. Burman came clucking. And Mrs. Brown came running with a great bottle of "Liniment for Injured Limbs."

But when they got Mr. Miser on his feet, it was plain that it would take more than liniment to mend him. They carried him into his house and laid him on a very dusty couch. The ladies all bustled around and looked for clean cloths and hot water. And Mr. Snoopstagel, pushing his bicycle, went off for the doctor.

AND THAT WAS how Mr. Miser's pumpkin vine got away from him. It grew and it grew and it grew in every direction. In every yard in which it grew it bore pumpkins. The little green balls spread and swelled into big green balls. Finally, the green balls grew into round orange-colored pumpkins. And they grew in every yard but Mr. Miser's.

All this time poor Mr. Miser had his foot bound up in plaster and rags. He could do nothing but sit on the porch and watch his vine running away. The more it ran the more sour and disagreeable Mr. Hermit Miser got. How he hated the thought of his beautiful golden pumpkins being eaten by other people!

It made him feel maddest of all because there were no pumpkins inside his own fence. If he were going to have any, he would have to go and get them back from his neighbors. And he hadn't spoken to his neighbors in years, except to scold Mrs. Burman about keeping the vine in her yard.

The summer went by and the days began to get too chilly for Mr. Hermit Miser to sit on the porch. The pumpkins got so ripe and yellow they looked as if they would burst. Mr. Miser got so thin and yellow — because of all the jealous thoughts that were stewing around in him — that he looked as if he would burst.

One night there was a frost. The next morning Mr. Miser hobbled out into the yard and looked over the south fence at Mrs. Burman's pumpkin. He thought of how good it would taste in a big round pie. He couldn't bear to look at it too long, so he hobbled over to the east fence. There he saw that Mrs. Brown had two pumpkins in her yard.

And then he saw that Miss Pitcher had two in her yard and that out in the road, along the ditch, there were three more yellow pumpkins! Angrily he went back to the house and chased the cat. Then he sat down and began to worry about how he could get his pumpkins back.

"By rights," thought Mr. Miser, gritting his teeth, "they should all be mine!"

Mr. Miser walked all around his yard. He looked at all his runaway pumpkins. He worried all morning. He was so busy worrying that he forgot to eat any lunch. And he worried all afternoon.

Then, just as it began to get dark, he decided what he would do. He would wait until it was as black as the inside of a hat. Then he would crawl through the fence and he'd get his pumpkin from Mrs. Burman's yard.

So when it was dark he blew out his candle and went out of his rackety-packety house and closed the door behind him. He walked quietly through the yard and up to the fence.

Then Mr. Hermit Miser got down and slid through the hole in the fence. It was very dark and the tall leaves of the pumpkin vine scratched him. But Mr. Hermit Miser was too excited to think. He kept reaching out here and there. He was feeling for the big smooth round pumpkin that he had seen that very morning, shining like gold in the sun.

But he couldn't find it. He crawled and he felt, and he felt and he crawled. But still he couldn't find the pumpkin.

At last he decided that he would start crawling close to the fence from one end of the garden to the other. Then when he got there he would crawl back again (just a few inches farther over) to the *other* end of the garden. And when he got *there* he would crawl back again (just a few inches farther over) to the *other* end of the garden. And if he did that until he had been all over the garden, like a man plowing, he couldn't miss such a big thing as the pumpkin.

SO, Mr. Hermit Miser crawled. And he crawled and he crawled and he CRAWLED. And still he couldn't find the pumpkin. His hands got very sore and sticky — because he was squashing the vine. His face was hot and prickly. His knees were stiff and creaking. But still he couldn't find the pumpkin.

Mr. Miser crawled until it seemed to him that he had crawled all night. He must have crawled over that garden a dozen times. At last he had to admit that the pumpkin just couldn't be there. So he picked himself up and went home.

Mr. Hermit Miser was as mad as *hops*!

The next morning bright and early he got up and went to look over Mrs. Burman's fence. There lay the pumpkin vine, all trampled and mashed. And there stood Mrs. Burman, looking as if she had a great joke all to herself.

"Looks as if some strange animal got in here last night," she said out loud to nobody. "It's a blessing I harvested my pumpkin crop yesterday."

At that Mr. Hermit Miser made a noise like something blowing up and went galloping back to his own porch again.

But after Mrs. Burman had gone into her own house he went and looked at Miss Pitcher's pumpkins. He noticed just where they grew. Next, he went and looked at Mrs. Brown's pumpkins and he noticed just where *they* grew.

Then Mr. Hermit Miser said. "Hm! I'll sit on my porch and I'll watch all day. I'll get those pumpkins tonight if I never do another thing! And in the meantime I'll get the pumpkins out of the street. I *know* I can get *them*!"

So he walked out and picked the three pumpkins which grew near the ditch. Then he carried them back, one at a time, into his own house.

He felt a great deal better after this. He sat on the porch and watched the other pumpkins and he felt almost happy.

But the trouble was that Miss Pitcher lived on one side of Mr. Hermit Miser and Mrs. Brown lived behind him. So he had to get up and move and watch one of the gardens a while. Then he moved back and watched the other garden a while. He just couldn't watch both gardens at once.

At last it got dark and Mr. Hermit Miser climbed over the fence into Miss Pitcher's garden. He walked straight to the place where he had seen the pumpkins — but they weren't there any more!

He jumped up and down all over Miss Pitcher's part of the vine. Then he ran to his own back yard and jumped over Mrs. Brown's fence. He went straight to the place where *her* pumpkins were — but *they* weren't there any longer, either.

And then Mr. Miser was mad! He went home and slammed the door. He slammed it so hard that all the windowpanes that were left in the window in the front of his house fell out with a crash. This frightened the cat, who humped her back and spat and ran up a tree. Mr. Miser was so mad that he forgot to eat any supper. He just sat in a chair all night and shivered and shook with the cold from the broken windows.

When morning came he felt very sad to think he had lost all but three of the pumpkins. He went and looked at them. The pumpkins were so round and yellow and bright and *cheerful* looking that they made him feel better right away.

"I'll have some pumpkin pies anyway," thought Mr. Hermit Miser, "and I'll eat every crumb of them myself. I'll not give anybody a single bite!"

So he set out to make himself some pumpkin pies. He had never made a pumpkin pie, but he thought he could do it with a little planning.

He mixed some dough — out of flour and water and a little salt — and he slapped it and he pounded it until it lay flat. Then he laid it in a pan. He set the pumpkin in the middle of it and popped it into the oven.

Then he remembered that somewhere he had read, "Sprinkle generously with sugar." He didn't like to do anything generously, but he did want a good pumpkin pie. So he put a whole handful of sugar right on top of the pumpkin, and then he put it back into the oven.

Mr. Hermit Miser pulled his chair up in front of the stove and sat down to wait for his pie to cook.

Soon a most delightful smell began to come out of the oven and Mr. Hermit Miser took a deep breath. Then he looked over towards Mrs. Burman's house and frowned. There was a truly delightful smell coming from Mrs. Burman's house, but Mr. Miser couldn't smell it because the smell in his own house was getting stronger and *stronger* and *stronger*.

And it wasn't so delightful now.

It smelled like something burning.

Mr. Hermit Miser got worried. It had been so long since he had cooked something in the oven that he thought perhaps he had forgotten how baking smells.

So he waited a little while longer.

But not much longer, because soon the smell got so strong that he couldn't stand it.

So he opened the door of the oven.

Oh, my!

There was the dough — hard and white — like stone. And there was the pumpkin, sort of wilted, and the sugar all black and smoking.

Mr. Miser had a *fit*!

He grabbed a towel. He grabbed the pie. And he rushed to the door and threw it out. Then he sat down and got hopping mad all over again.

But there were still two pumpkins left, and Mr. Hermit Miser was determined to have a pie. So he sat down and he thought and thought. At last he remembered that to make a pie you must cut up the pumpkin and cook it first.

When he remembered this, he jumped up. He stumbled over the cat as he rushed to the pantry to get another pumpkin. It was a huge pumpkin.

He got a knife and cut the pumpkin in half. He cut it into little chunks. He cut off the hard rind and put the chunks in a bucket. Presently the bucket was full, so he got the dishpan. When that was full he got the saucepans. When they were full he still had some of the pumpkin left. He was very, very tired and felt that he never wanted to see a pumpkin again as long as he lived! So he went to bed.

The next morning he started on the pumpkin cutting again. He filled the coal scuttle and the scrap basket. He even had to put some pumpkin in his hat. And he still had to cook it and make the dough and bake the pie.

This time when he made the dough he stewed the pumpkin that was in the dishpan. He put a lot of sugar in it. Then he put it in the oven.

He pulled his chair up in front of the stove and sat down to wait.

Nothing happened. Not a thing.

Mr. Miser had forgotten to build a fire!

When he had opened the oven door for about the one hundredth time and the pie wasn't cooked, he suddenly knew what the matter was. So he built the fire. He built a good one because he was simply starving and he could hardly wait to taste the pie.

He built such a good fire that the stove got red hot and the pie burned to a crisp.

Well — Mr. Miser worked for seven and a half days on those pumpkin pies and he never did make one. He tried frying them and broiling them. He baked them in saucers and he baked them in bread pans. He mashed the pumpkin and he put it through the food chopper. But it still didn't make a pie.

The house was gummy with pumpkin. By this time Mr. Miser had taken on a sort of coat of pumpkin where little bits had stuck all over him.

He'd used up all three of his pumpkins by now, and still he didn't have a pumpkin pie.

When the last pie came out of the oven and looked worse than the first, Mr. Miser just cried. He went out on the back steps and sat down. He put his head on his knees, threw his apron over his head, and cried.

When Mrs. Burman looked out of her kitchen window and saw Mr. Hermit Miser crying, she dropped a pan of potatoes and said, "Mercy me!"

Almost at the same time Miss Pitcher looked out of her window and saw Mr. Miser crying and she said, "Well, forever more!"

Both of them ran out of their back gates to Mrs. Brown, who said, "It's never so!"

Then all three went and stood in front of Mr. Miser and said, "Hem!"

When Mr. Miser heard them say, "Hem!" he knew that they had seen him crying. He was so ashamed that he wouldn't take his head from under his apron. He just sat up with the apron over his face and said gruffly, "What do you want? Get out!"

But Mrs. Burman and Mrs. Brown had seen the pumpkin pies — dozens of them — which Mr. Hermit Miser had thrown out into the yard.

Miss Pitcher was staring at the simply awful mess that was Mr. Miser's kitchen. Suddenly the three friends looked at one another and shook their heads. They looked very sad for a minute, and then very glad for another. Then they all put their hands over their mouths because they were smiling.

And Mrs. Burman said, "Tck! Tck! What a shame to have wasted all those pumpkins! What were you trying to do with them?"

"I was making a pie!" said Mr. Miser, and his voice was stuffy with tears and apron. "I wanted a pumpkin pie!"

And in spite of himself he began to cry again.

"He's all worn out!" said Mrs. Burman. "And no wonder! All that work and nothing to show for it!"

"And his pumpkins all wasted!" said Mrs. Brown. "And such tasty ones, too!"

"His kitchen!" sighed Miss Pitcher. "Why, I made pumpkin pies in mine and you'd never know it."

"You made a pie?" asked Mr. Hermit Miser, just letting one eye show from behind the apron.

"A lot of them," said Miss Pitcher, "all as smooth and spicy and fine as you'd hope to see."

"Such flavor that pumpkin had. I've already eaten two of mine." And Mrs. Brown sighed. "I don't believe I ever made such crust!"

"Were they spicy?" asked Mr. Miser, wiping his eyes on the apron.

"Umm!" said Mrs. Brown.

"And sort of cracked across the top? And brown and custardy?" asked Mr. Miser, his voice trembling.

"Mine were," said Mrs. Burman. "With the pumpkin just drawing away from the crust. Ummmm!" And she winked at Mrs. Brown.

"I — can't stand it!" wept Mr. Miser. "Everybody has a pie but me — and they were my pumpkins!"

He was just ready to jump up and down in one of his rages when Mrs. Burman said, "Listen, Mr. Miser. How would you like a big, big slice of nice golden-brown pie? After all, they were your pumpkins and I think you should have them back. But they're made into pies now and we made the pies. They've got our eggs and butter . . ."

"Oh, do you put eggs and butter in them?" asked Mr. Miser, surprised.

Mrs. Burman nodded. "And sugar and spice and lots of good rich milk . . ."

"And a little salt to set all that off," said Miss Pitcher.

"No wonder . . ." said Mr. Hermit Miser, and his eyes filled with tears again.

"Now listen here," said Mrs. Burman. "You can have your pumpkins — all made into pies, too, if you'll do a few things to get them."

"What?" asked Mr. Miser eagerly.

"Well, that fence between your yard and mine — it needs mending and it needs painting."

"I'll do it!" said Mr. Miser.

"And your house needs the same," said Mrs. Brown.

"I'll — I'll fix that, too," said Mr. Miser weakly.

"And the cat—" said Miss Pitcher.

And all three said, "Yes, that cat! You'll have to feed it and wash the front step so the cat will have a place to sun itself."

"All right!" said Mr. Miser sulkily. "When do I get my pies?"

"When you've done all that!" said the three.

"WHAT? You mean I can't have my pies until I've mended the fence and painted the house and fattened the cat and . . ."

"We'll help you!" said Mrs. Brown. "We'll help you and all the neighbors will help you."

"The neighbors don't like me," said Mr. Hermit Miser, and hung his head.

"They will — if you like them," said Mrs. Brown. "Come on."

And so the neighbors came. They cleaned and painted the house inside and out. They mended the windows and scrubbed the steps. They cleaned up the yard and they fed the cat with cream and fish. They bought new pots and pans, all green and white, for Mr. Miser's kitchen. They even brought him a cook book!

Last of all they brought the pies over. There were dozens and dozens of round, spicy, sweet, crusty pumpkin pies. The neighbors laid them out on tables all through the house.

When Mr. Miser saw them he said, "I never could eat all these pies in years and years. I guess my neighbors will have to keep on helping me."

And so they did. They ate pie and they ate pie and ate pie, until there was just one left. Mr. Miser put it on his pantry shelf for breakfast.

And when they left Mr. Miser said, "I never, never again will let my house get shabby and dirty. I never, never will let my fence go broken and unpainted. And I never, never will be mad at anybody again. Thank you!"

And everybody cheered.

Then they all went away. Mr. Hermit Miser sat by his fire with his cat — which was purring.

The freshly painted little house was neat and clean. But it was not painted green and white, like all the other houses in Gillygreen Lane. Oh, no. It was bright yellow with green shutters, like a pumpkin with leaves, because Mr. Hermit Miser said that he never wanted to forget that it had been his pumpkin vine which had made his neighbors into friends.

Mr. Miser certainly needed help with his pies, didn't he? Well, if you ever want to make a pie, or muffins, or even a pot of pumpkin soup, maybe these recipes will help you. (There is also a poem and some interesting pie history at the end, too.)

Visit SmidgenPress.com/pumpkin-recipes for a print-at-home recipe PDF. Special thanks to the Burns family, Heather-Lei, Kathryn S., and Zonya G. for your input on these hundred-year-old selections.

Sturdy Pie Crust
with egg and milk

INGREDIENTS

2 cups flour
½ tsp. salt
⅔ cup shortening

1 egg, beaten
enough milk to make ½ cup
see note in recipe

MAKE IT

Stir together the flour and salt.

Cut in shortening using two knives or a pastry cutter until lumps are roughly the size of large peas.

Crack an egg into a measuring cup, beat, and add milk to make ½ cup total liquid. Stir liquid slowly into flour mixture until mixture almost holds together, then pack with hands and place on floured surface. Roll out, place in pie plate, and use as directed.

Fluffy Pumpkin Pie
with beaten egg whites

INGREDIENTS

3 egg whites
¼ cup white sugar

3 egg yolks
¼ cup white sugar
1 Tbsp. flour
½ tsp. powdered ginger
½ tsp. cinnamon
¼ tsp. nutmeg
　or pumpkin pie spice
½ tsp. salt
2 cups pumpkin
1 Tbsp. butter, melted

½ cup milk, warmed
1 Tbsp. molasses

MAKE IT

Beat the egg whites until foamy, then add ¼ cup sugar and beat until stiff. In another bowl, mix egg yolks with dry ingredients, then add pumpkin and butter. Mix warm milk and molasses, then stir into pumpkin. Fold pumpkin carefully in with egg whites (batter will be streaky).

Spread into unbaked pie crust and bake at 350º F (180º C) about 45-55 minutes, until only slightly jiggly and nicely browned.

Adapted from *Table Talk*, November 1914

Pumpkin Pie
with butter and molasses

INGREDIENTS

1 cup milk, warmed

2 Tbsp. molasses

—

1 ½ cups pumpkin

½ cup sugar

2 eggs, beaten

1 tsp. cinnamon

1 tsp. ginger

½ tsp. salt

2 Tbsp. butter, melted

MAKE IT

Stir molasses into warm milk. Mix into remaining ingredients. Pour into unbaked pie pastry and bake at 350º F (180º C) about 45 minutes.

Adapted from *The Boston Cooking-School Magazine*, December 1913

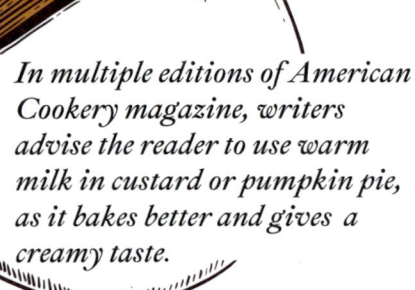

In multiple editions of American Cookery magazine, writers advise the reader to use warm milk in custard or pumpkin pie, as it bakes better and gives a creamy taste.

Fancy Pie Crust
for squash or pumpkin pies

Hint: parchment paper can help with cleanup. If you can find "freezer tape," this will stick to the parchment to anchor the corners to the countertop and can withstand a few minutes of gentle rolling.

INGREDIENTS

1 ¼ cups flour

¼ tsp. salt

¼ tsp. baking powder

—

2 Tbsp. sugar

½ cup shortening or butter

—

1 egg yolk

1 Tbsp. lemon juice

1 ½ Tbsp. water

MAKE IT

Stir or sift dry ingredients together. Cut in shortening or butter with knives or pastry cutter. Add the egg yolk, lemon juice, and water, and gently combine.

Roll on floured surface and place carefully into pie plate. Bake as pie recipe directs.

Adapted from *Cakes, Pastry & Dessert Dishes*, 1917

Pumpkin or Squash Muffins
good to serve with soup

INGREDIENTS

⅔ cup pumpkin

1 cup milk (any kind)

—

¼ cup sugar

2 eggs, beaten

—

2 ¾ cups flour

1 tsp. salt

pinch of nutmeg

3 tsp. baking powder

—

2 Tbsp. butter, melted

MAKE IT

Mix the milk and pumpkin or squash, then add sugar and eggs. Mix together the flour, salt, nutmeg, and baking powder, then add dry ingredients to the milk mixture. Add melted butter and mix gently.

Divide into muffin pans, greased or with cupcake papers, and bake at 350º F (180º C) for 30 minutes.

"Cheese is usually served with apple pie, mince pie and pumpkin pie. If you wish to give the pie a more festive look, shape a package of cream cheese in the form of tiny apples and place one on each individual dish with the pie."

American Cookery, February 1927

Adapted from *Table Talk* magazine, November 1914

Pumpkin Corn Bread

INGREDIENTS

1 cup cornmeal
1 tsp. baking soda
1 ½ tsp. baking powder

1 cup boiling water
½ cup cornmeal

1 cup buttermilk
   *or soured milk; see note
1 cup pumpkin or squash
2 eggs, beaten
1 tsp. salt

1 Tbsp. sugar
1 Tbsp. butter, melted

MAKE IT

Mix 1 cup of cornmeal with baking soda and baking powder.

Scald the other ½ cup of cornmeal with the boiling water, then stir in with the buttermilk, pumpkin, eggs, salt, and the dry cornmeal mixture.

Lastly, add in the sugar and melted butter and beat until it's a light batter. Spread in a 9x9 pan and bake at 425° F (220° C) for 20-30 minutes.

Pumpkin Fritters

INGREDIENTS

1 egg, beaten until slightly foamy
½ cup milk
1 ¼ tsp. salt
1 Tbsp. olive oil
1 cup flour
1 cup pumpkin
pinch of red pepper (optional)

MAKE IT

Mix all ingredients until batter is smooth and glossy.

Drop spoonfuls into frying pan with very hot oil, or deep fry.

Cook for 8 minutes or until golden. Drain on paper towels and serve hot.

*To sour milk, put 1 Tbsp. vinegar or lemon juice into a measuring cup and fill with milk to make 1 cup. Stir and let stand at least 5 minutes.

Adapted from *Table Talk* magazine, November 1914

Pumpkin or Squash Soup

INGREDIENTS

1 medium onion, chopped

1 cup chopped celery

3 Tbsp. butter/margarine

3 Tbsp. flour

4 cups broth or stock
   beef, chicken, or vegetable

2 cups pumpkin or squash

Salt, pepper, and paprika
   to taste

1 bay leaf (optional)

1 blade mace (optional)

1 cup milk (any kind) or cream

2 Tbsp. butter/margarine

½ cup cream, whipped (optional)
   for garnish at serving time

MAKE IT

Sauté the onion and celery in 3 Tbsp. of the butter for 5-10 minutes, until soft but not brown.

Add the flour to create a paste.

Then add broth, pumpkin, and seasonings, and cook over medium heat for at least 10 minutes, stirring occasionally.

Add in milk or cream. Stir in the remaining 2 Tbsp. butter.

Remove from heat. Garnish with whipped cream before serving.

Adapted from *Table Talk* magazine, November 1914

Pumpkin-in-the-Shell

There's a certain charm in
   cook books,
And the reader's hunger swells
As he lingers over Grandma's,
And the secrets that it tells.

Grandma's was a portly volume;
Every recipe set down
In her fine Italian writing,
Faded now to leafy brown.

How one's mouth begins to water;
How one longs to taste again
Muster gingerbread and tartlets,
Currant buns and doughnut men!

But one dish described by Grandma
Never verse its charm could tell;
Never words describe its savor–
It was Pumpkin-in-the-Shell.

Take a pumpkin, golden yellow,
Cut a slice from off the top;
With a spoon scrape out the fiber,
And the seeds for next year's crop.

In the hollow sprinkle honey;
Fill with milk of long ago,
Not the stuff of modern
   commerce,
But a milk of creamy flow.

Scatter spices, bear the vessel
To the oven's glowing heat;
Watch and pray and keep the fire
Till the product is complete.

Here it comes, a globe of
   sunshine!
Lift the cover, smell the spice;
Not a dish on Nero's menus
Ever tasted half so nice!

—*Nora Archibald Smith*

The Ancestry of Certain Pies
or, why are a Boston Cream Pie and an Apple Pie both pie?

Oliver Wendell Holmes once asserted that he liked genuine pie, but added that he was not patriotic enough to like that named for the father of his country who, according to the New England poet's belief, was not first in pies. This brings up the question of the origin of this sort of cousin to real pie. For a long time the home cook and the baker vied in making what they called "Washington pies," and years ago this sort of cross between cake and pie was considered part of a supper or tea which in many homes took the place of the now customary six o'clock dinner.

Not long ago I asked an old southern housewife how a thin two-layer cake happened to be called a pie. Her answer was that during the Civil War the housewives at the capital city were hard pressed for pie material, and to understand the inconvenience of this condition it should be remembered that the southern states were and still are as strong for pie as the New England section of the country ever was. The pie belt is really broad enough to reach from the Canadian line to the Gulf states so far as the East is concerned.

Washington city was so besieged during the war that green stuff for pie filling was at a premium, and sometimes could not be secured at all. Hence the pie in its usual form was almost impossible. However, the cooks baked a thin cake batter in two round, very shallow tins, and between these cakes they spread jelly or preserves in a thin coating.

Of course one could not imagine a southern housekeeper, even in war time, to be in such straits that her preserve closet was bare. The semblance of pie was thus made. . . . It was toothsome, even if it had to be presented as "something just as good," which injures the reputation of anything in these days of resentment towards substitutes. The good qualities of Washington pie spread elsewhere, and any northern man or woman who will acknowledge to living sixty-odd years can remember when it became the fashion for dessert. It was never iced but the top was dusted with powdered sugar and sometimes the sugar was sifted from a paper cornucopia in lines to represent a lattice of narrow strips of pastry.

One reason that this cake-pie has lost favor may be the depths to which it sunk in the hands of the bakers who made it of mock sponge cake made light with baking powder and colored artificially to appear as if many eggs were used in it. The filling often would be of cheap commercial raspberry jam which, until the pure food laws were enforced, was made of glucose, coloring and hayseed. The tradition that New Englanders eat pie for breakfast has some foundation, although the custom went into discard long ago. Ralph Waldo Emerson ate pie at his morning meal and resented the inquiry as to why he did so by asking in true Yankee style, "But what is pie for but to eat?" In his day the morning meal was hearty if not always well chosen. Hot mince pie was as certain at breakfast a good part of the year as grapefruit and cereal now are. . . .

Mince pies date back centuries ago and to the Christmas custom of baking a crust in an oblong dish to represent the manger in which the Holy Child was laid. They were then called shred pies. In time mince pies were succeeded at Christmas by plum pudding, which yet remains the holiday dessert.

Apple pie is known to be older than the settling of this country, and apple trees were planted early in the colonies. . . . Fresh apple pies should be served while slightly warm, as by the advice of the noted preacher, Henry Ward Beecher, who like the judge of colonial days was a "good trencher man." Apple pie is a favorite at the lunch counter, and if of good quality it seems like painting the lily to "ice the apple." And here it may not be out of place to recall the supposed origin of the saying, "in apple pie order." Away back in early times when twenty to thirty apple pies were baked in the brick oven on Saturday they were set on shelves in the "butt'y," as the pantry was then called. They were arranged so many for each day, and it was nearly a household sin to eat pies from the wrong shelf or out of their prescribed order.

Pumpkins or pompions were among the most common and cheapest food materials of the early New England settlements. In a lean season, if need be, a pie could be made by sprinkling a greased plate with rye meal and filling it with stewed and seasoned pumpkin rightly diluted with milk, which was generally about a penny a quart. In times of plenty these pies were made with cream and eggs and foreign spices. . . .

The glamour of the past cannot make us long for stale pastry, and if the best of home cooking is not within reach the food shop pie, freshly baked and in its paper frill, looks most inviting from the window display of ready-to-eats. Pie in some form seems to have been a human need for at least five hundred years.

—Alice E. Whitaker
American Cookery, October 1925

Want to connect with us?

We hope you've enjoyed this pumpkin-filled book. Here are some ways to come join our "neighborhood."

Join our newsletter: SmidgenPress.com/newsletter
Facebook/Instagram/TikTok: @SmidgenPress
Request a book: SmidgenPress.com/requests
Email our team: hello@smidgenpress.com

Or visit us at SmidgenPress.com to see more of our unique editions.

The Daisy Chain
  Charlotte Mary Yonge

The Fortunes of Philippa
  Angela Brazil

Frankenstein
  Mary Wollstonecraft Shelley
  illus. Carl Lagerquist

A Narrative of the Negro
  Leila Amos Pendleton

The Prisoner of Zenda
  Anthony Hope

The Real Fairy Folk
  Louise Jamison
  illus. James Gleeson

The Story of the Other Wise Man
  Henry van Dyke
  illus. J.R. Flanagan

The Voyagers
  Padraic Colum

Made in United States
Troutdale, OR
10/08/2023

13529504R00040